Our Liberty Bell

by HENRY JONAS MAGAZINER

illustrated by JOHN O'BRIEN

HOLIDAY HOUSE / New York

To my beloved Margery
H. J. M.

For Tess
J. O.

Library of Congress Cataloging-in-Publication Data
Magaziner, Henry Jonas.
Our Liberty bell / by Henry Jonas Magaziner ; illustrated by John O'Brien.— 1st ed.
p. cm.
Includes bibliographical references.
ISBN-10: 0-8234-1892-8 (hardcover)
1. Liberty Bell—Juvenile literature. 2. Philadelphia (Pa.) —
Buildings, structures, etc.—Juvenile literature. I. O'Brien, John, 1953– II. Title.
F158.8.I3M34 2005
974.8'11—dc22
2004054196
ISBN-13: 978-0-8234-1892-3 (hardcover)
ISBN-13: 978-0-8234-2081-0 (paperback)
ISBN-10: 0-8234-2081–7 (paperback)

CONTENTS

1. The Bell Is Born   5

2. Important News   9

3. When Our Country
Was Young   18

4. Darkness, Then Light   21

5. The Liberty Bell Helped
Other Important Causes   26

6. Our Liberty Bell Today   28

Glossary   30

Author's Note   31

Index   32

1.
THE BELL IS BORN

It was 1752.

They, the members of the Pennsylvania Assembly, must have been pleased. After waiting for more than nine months, the bell they had ordered from English bell makers had finally arrived in Philadelphia.

On behalf of the Assembly, Isaac Norris, the Quaker who was its speaker, had ordered the bell in 1751. It was to be part of the fiftieth-anniversary celebration of the 1701 Charter of Privileges, which William Penn, Pennsylvania's founder, had granted to the Pennsylvania colonists. That charter had guaranteed religious freedom, an elected assembly, and traditional English liberties. Penn, an ardent believer in such rights, had proclaimed, "The public must and will be served." He expected a community of brotherly love to develop—tolerant, free, secure, and, above all, peaceful. It was those very qualities that attracted many colonists to settle in Pennsylvania, one of the thirteen British colonies in North America.

Since the bell was to celebrate the golden anniversary of the

Pennsylvania charter, which pledged liberties, Norris had ordered the bell makers to put this biblical inscription on it: "Proclaim Liberty thro' all the Land to all the inhabitants thereof. Levit. XXV 10."

Now that the bell had arrived, the assemblymen planned to hang it in the tower of the Pennsylvania State House, in Philadelphia. There it would call people together to hear town criers announce important news. No one yet had invented radio or television, so the colonists depended on the town criers for their news.

The assemblymen rang the bell to hear its tone. It made a dull, unpleasant sound. Then it cracked! Of course they were angry, so they decided to return it to England. When they contacted the captain of the English ship then in port, he refused to take it aboard. One assemblyman pointed out that even if they could return the bell, they would have to wait another six months for a new one. And that one might crack! They decided to ask local bell makers John Pass and John Stow to cast a new, stronger bell.

△ △ △

Pass and Stow must have been both challenged and pleased to have been selected to make that very special bell. They took the cracked English bell to their foundry, a place where metal is cast, and, using clay and manure, made an inner and an outer mold from it. The molds fitted over each other, leaving a void that was the exact thickness, size, and shape of the bell they were going to cast. (It was like inverting a small flowerpot and putting a larger inverted flowerpot over it.) The biblical inscription to go on the bell was cut into the inside of the outer mold. This time the inscription read: "Proclaim LIBERTY throughout all the Land unto all the inhabitants thereof. Lev. XXV. X."

Next the bell makers broke up the English bell with a sledgehammer and threw all the chunks into a crucible. To make a stronger bell that would not crack, they added some copper to the mix. They heated the metals until they got so hot they melted and became liquid. Then they poured the liquid metals into the void between the two bell molds. (It was rather like pouring Jell-O water into a mold. However, unlike Jell-O water, the liquid metals from the crucible were extremely hot.) When the liquid cooled and became solid again, the foundry men removed it from the bell molds. They made a clapper to hang inside the bell. It would swing freely and hit the inside of the bell, making it ring. They had created a brand-new, handsome bell. They must have been proud when they took it to the State House.

So many people wanted to hear the new bell ring that the assembly-men arranged to have a big picnic in the park behind the State House. Everyone came. However, when the bellman rang the bell, the crowd was horrified. People covered their ears. The bell's sound was dreadful!

Imagine how John Pass and John Stow must have felt. They quickly took the new bell back to their foundry, broke it up, and threw the pieces into the crucible. To make a bell with a better tone, they added some tin and a tiny bit of silver to the mix. Then they followed the same procedure as before. When the liquid metals cooled and became solid again, a bell a little more than three feet high and weighing 2,080 pounds had been produced. While it had some unevenness on its outer face, it was still

a beautiful bell,

with a pleasant tone,

with the famous biblical inscription on it.

Since the sound of the new bell was much better, the Assembly had it hung from a yoke that would hold the bell and allow it to swing for ringing. The yoke was made from an American elm tree. Finally, the Assembly had the bell hoisted to the wooden upper part of the State House bell tower.

By June 1753 the bell was all set for its big job.

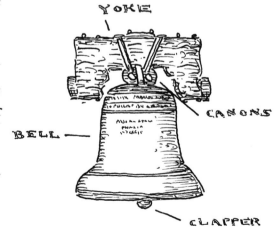

8

2.
IMPORTANT NEWS

The bell's job was to assemble people to hear about important happenings and events, and in 1763 it rang joyfully. The town crier told everyone that the treaty ending the French and Indian War had been signed. The British had won.

In spring 1764 the bell rang to protest the British-imposed Sugar Act tax. The colonists feared that the tax would destroy their economy. They said it was "taxation without representation." Later the colonists also resented Britain's Stamp Act, which forced them to buy tax stamps to put on all legal papers and many other printed items. Several colonists threatened the stamp agent physically and he promptly resigned. That autumn the bell rang and the town crier announced that the Pennsylvania Assembly had sent Benjamin Franklin to London to try to end that tax.

In October 1765 the bell rang mournfully, and all who assembled learned that the British ship *Royal Charlotte* was sailing up the Delaware River to Philadelphia, bearing tax stamps. One group of citizens was so angry, it gathered in the London Coffee House and, with ceremony, *burned* Stamp Act documents!

In March 1770 the bellman rang the State House bell and the town crier told Philadelphians about the "Boston Massacre." A crowd of protesting colonists had gathered in front of the customs house in Boston. British soldiers fired into the crowd, killing or wounding eleven people. The first one to die was Crispus Attucks, a black man.

In December 1773 the Pennsylvania State House bellman rang the bell so that all could hear about the Boston Tea Party. A group of Boston colonists had devised a very daring plan to oppose the tea tax. Dressed as Native Americans, the men had boarded three tea ships belonging to the British East India Company. Once on board, they dumped 342 chests of the ships' tea into Boston's harbor.

When they heard that news, some Philadelphians shouted, "Bravo!"

It took weeks for news of the Tea Party to reach the British Parliament, but once it did, parliament reacted very firmly. It closed Boston's harbor. After Paul Revere, a Boston silversmith, rode down to Philadelphia with the news, the bellman rang the State House bell and the town crier told everyone about Boston's plight. That convinced many colonists that the British were bullying them and that they should revolt against England. Later the bellman rang the bell and the town crier told everyone that many of the other British colonies had rallied to aid Boston. Consequently, Philadelphians decided to raise money to help that suffering city.

By 1774 many British North American colonists, like the Tea

Party Bostonians, were enraged with England's King George III, who was taking away more and more of their liberties. A group of leading colonists, from twelve of the thirteen British colonies, decided to meet in Philadelphia.

Since they were plotting against the king, these men, called Patriots, had to keep their meetings top secret. So they gathered in a secluded location, Carpenters' Hall, which was up a passageway away from the street. Many Patriots who would later become leaders of our nation attended those meetings. During one session, Virginia delegate Patrick Henry stood up and shouted, "The distinctions between Virginians, Pennsylvanians, New Yorkers, and New Englanders are no more. I am not a Virginian, but an American!"

The Patriots made some extraordinary decisions in Carpenters' Hall. To force the British to change their policies, which were limiting the freedom of colonial trade, the Patriots determined to stop all trading with England. They also agreed to meet again if King George did not address their grievances. Since they were deciding on actions to take against the British—actions that could cause them to be "hanged by the neck"—they told the bellman *not* to ring the bell to announce their meetings.

Today, historians call those meetings the *First* Continental Congress.

In April 1775 the bellman rang the bell and the town crier told all that there had been a skirmish with the British at Lexington, Massachusetts. Eight colonists had been killed. Although no war yet had been declared, the War of Independence had actually started.

Beginning in May 1775 the *Second* Continental Congress met in Philadelphia for 148 days. This time everything was *very* different. The delegates had decided on their course. They wanted no more secrecy, so they met in the Pennsylvania State House. They set up the Continental army and appointed George Washington to be its commander in chief. That was very important news and meant that the movement for freedom from England was growing. Patrick Henry had said in March, "I know not what course others may take; but as for me, give me liberty or give me death." Now the delegates wanted the bell to ring so that everyone could hear about the many important decisions they were making. They wanted everyone's support for liberty.

Of course, some people did not agree with opposing King George. Those British Loyalists, called Tories, were worried. They were nervous about how King George would respond to the actions the delegates were taking. They were afraid the colonists could lose *all* their rights. They wanted the delegates to leave things alone. However, most people did not agree with the Tories, and the Patriots in the congress continued organizing the rebellion. They had the bell rung to tell everyone about their decisions.

Later, working with four other members of the congress, Thomas Jefferson, of Virginia, wrote the Declaration of Independence. It began by explaining the desire to separate the colonies from England. Next it asserted "that all men are created equal" and that all were entitled to "life, liberty and the pursuit of happiness." It listed the many grievances the colonists had against King George, such as

"imposing taxes on us without our consent." Finally, it declared the thirteen colonies liberated from British rule and asserted that they were now "free and independent states" permitted to do what all nations do!

John Hancock, who had chaired the congress, signed the Declaration of Independence with a large, bold signature and said, "There! King George can read *that* without his spectacles." Then all the other members of the congress signed it.

John Adams wrote home to his wife: "Yesterday the greatest question was decided which ever was debated in America; and a greater perhaps never was, nor will be, decided among men. A resolution was passed without one dissenting colony, that 'these United Colonies are, and of Right ought to be, Free and Independent States.'"

How brave those Patriots were!

On July 8, 1776, the Patriots had the bellman ring the bell for a long, long time to make sure that everyone would gather. After a huge crowd assembled, a Patriot read the entire Declaration of Independence to them. America had declared its freedom and the War of Independence was spreading. All of Philadelphia's bells rang, people lit bonfires, and everywhere there were demonstrations of joy.

Later, the State House bell rang to announce that three leading Patriots had picked *E Pluribus Unum* as the national motto. It is Latin for "Out of Many, One." It meant that the thirteen former British colonies in America were going to act together, as one. Thomas Jefferson and John Adams, two of the Patriots who had picked that motto, later became U.S. presidents. Franklin, the third Patriot on the committee, is reputed to have said, "We must indeed all hang together, or, most assuredly, we shall all hang separately."

Meanwhile, King George responded to the Declaration of Independence by sending troops to America to crush the rebellion.

On Christmas night 1776, General Washington and his army crossed the Delaware River from Pennsylvania into Trenton, New Jersey. There they captured the sleeping Hessian soldiers, whom the British had hired to fight for them. Of course, the bellman rang the bell and the town crier announced that great news.

The bellman rang the bell on June 14, 1777, and the town crier told all who gathered that the congress had adopted a flag for the United States that had thirteen stripes and thirteen stars, standing for the thirteen former British colonies. (Since then a star has been

added every time another state has joined the Union.)

Later in 1777, British General William Howe's army was approaching Philadelphia. It had won the battles of Brandywine and Paoli, both near the city, so in September a group of Philadelphia Patriots held a meeting. They were worried. If the British were to take the city, they might take the bells from the State House and the churches and melt them down. Then they could recast the bells' metal into cannon to use against the Continental army.

They decided to take the bells to Allen's Town (today called Allentown), sixty miles away, and hide them. They felt that the British wouldn't look for them there.

All agreed.

While the Patriots were preparing the State House bell for the

trip, a boy saw them place it on a farm wagon and overheard where they were going to hide it. As the wagon pulled away, a Tory came along and asked the boy if he knew where they were taking the bell. Fortunately, that very smart boy did not tell him.

He probably saved the bell from being melted down again!

A horse-drawn wagon carried the bell. But the bell was much heavier than the crops usually put in the wagon, so the wagon eventually broke down. The Patriots were afraid that they would be caught before they could hide the bell from the British. Quickly, they found a stronger wagon, hoisted the bell onto it, and got it to Allen's Town safely.

They put the bell in a church basement along with Philadelphia's church bells. It remained there while the British occupied Philadelphia during the winter of 1777–1778.

Meanwhile, the colonists won the battle of Saratoga in New York. When the French heard that, they joined forces with the Patriots.

In June 1778 the British finally decided to leave Philadelphia and concentrate on occupying New York. So the Patriots returned all the bells to Philadelphia, and by late August all were rehung. Most Philadelphians must have been happy to have the bells returned and ringing again. However, back in 1774 many had complained that the State House bell had been ringing too often, so the Assembly had decided to have it ring for only the most important announcements.

In 1781 there was a most important announcement, so the State House bell rang and rang. America had won its freedom! Americans, along with the French, had mounted a campaign against the British at Yorktown, Virginia. British General Lord Charles Cornwallis finally had to surrender. The War of Independence was over. America was a free nation! When the crowd heard that great news, everyone rejoiced. People shouted and cheered. Some danced in the streets.

Since the bell rang for important occasions only, it certainly did ring in 1783 for another special announcement. The British had signed a treaty in Paris. They now agreed that the thirteen former colonies were no longer British possessions but were an independent nation, the United States of America.

3.
WHEN OUR COUNTRY WAS YOUNG

The bell rang in 1787 to announce that a group of leading citizens, including George Washington, James Madison, Benjamin Franklin, Alexander Hamilton, Robert Morris, and others, had gathered in Philadelphia and had drawn up a proposed constitution by which to govern our new nation. The town crier explained that the document made it clear that we would be a democracy. Instead of having a king rule us, we citizens would rule ourselves, through leaders we elect. The proposed constitution was sent to the thirteen states to vote on its adoption.

In 1788 the bellman rang and rang the bell and the town crier proclaimed that the states had adopted the Constitution! Later that year, the United States had its first election. Shortly thereafter the bellman rang the bell and the town crier announced that George Washington had been elected to be our first president.

In 1791 the bell rang and everyone assembled to hear that the states had voted to amend the Constitution. It now included the Bill of Rights!

Among the rights guaranteed:

We will have freedom of religion.

We will have free speech and a free press. The government will not tell us what we can say or print.

We will have trials by jury.

In 1792 the bellman rang the bell to gather everyone to hear that the people had elected George Washington to a second term as president.

In 1799 the bellman tolled the bell slowly and mournfully, as a funeral dirge. Sad news. That great American George Washington had died. Everyone mourned. Henry Lee read a eulogy on Washington, stating that Washington was "first in war, first in peace, first in the hearts of his fellow-citizens."

The next year the bellman rang the bell to announce that the government was moving from Philadelphia to a city on the Potomac River. Congress named that city Washington in honor of our first president. Later that year the bell was rung with some big news. The people had elected Thomas Jefferson president. He held the office from 1801 to 1809.

In 1803 the bellman rang the bell loud and long so that people could hear some thrilling news. President Jefferson had bought for us, from France, a vast area west of the Mississippi River. That land is called the Louisiana Purchase, and it just about doubled the size of our country. Today, all or parts of thirteen states are located in that area.

The bell hung in the State House tower for ninety-three years, and people used to climb up to see it and read its inscription. First it

hung in the upper part of the tower, which was built of wood. However, by 1781 that part of the tower had become wobbly and had to be torn down. So the bell was moved to the lower part of the tower, which was brick. (In 1828 the wooden part of the tower was rebuilt to the way it is today.)

Once the bell was relocated to the lower part of the tower, it was easier for people to climb up to see it. In 1835 someone who had seen the word *liberty* in the bell's inscription started calling the bell the Liberty Bell. By 1840 many people called it by that name.

Meanwhile, Pennsylvania moved its capital farther west in the state and the city of Philadelphia acquired the old State House, along with the Liberty Bell. Since the Declaration of Independence had been signed in the old State House, people started calling that building Independence Hall.

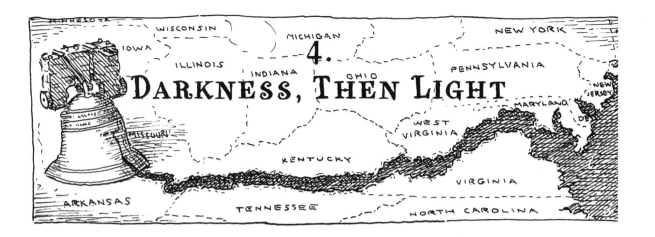

4.
DARKNESS, THEN LIGHT

George Washington was born on February 22, 1732, and became known as "the Father of Our Country." Every year after he died America celebrated his birthday on that date. In 1843, when the bellman rang the Liberty Bell as part of the celebration, it cracked. It was repaired, but three years later during the birthday celebration, it rang its last clear note. It cracked so badly that it could no longer ring! Although it hung silently in the tower, people still climbed up to see it. In 1852 Philadelphia officials had it taken down and then exhibited it near the statue of Washington in Independence Hall.

Twenty years earlier, in 1832, a number of women had formed the Boston Female Antislavery Society. These fighters against slavery, called abolitionists, wanted the slaves to gain their freedom. Just like everyone else, blacks should be at liberty to migrate to get jobs and to live with their families wherever they wished. Later, in 1837, the first female abolitionist convention was held in Philadelphia. While there the abolitionists discovered the Liberty Bell. Because of its inscription about liberty, they decided to make the Liberty Bell the symbol of their fight against slavery. New York's Anti-Slavery

Society pictured it on the cover of its magazine, named *Liberty*.

Abolitionists quoted Alexander Hamilton, who had written, "Natural liberty is the gift of the beneficent Creator of the whole human race."

Each year for twenty years beginning in 1839, Boston's antislavery activists, the Friends of Freedom, published another abolitionist booklet called *The Liberty Bell* to raise funds for their cause. They fused the Liberty Bell and its inscription with the Declaration of Independence.

In 1847 R. R. Marden, an abolitionist, wrote a poem entitled "The Liberty Bell":

Oh for a glorious peal at last,
Of the true Bell of Liberty!
To rend the air, and strike aghast,
The monster might of slavery.

By the 1850s abolitionists everywhere carried pictures of the Liberty Bell on banners in parades. They printed posters with its picture, always showing the crack.

The abolitionists decided to have a mass meeting against slavery in Independence Square, the park behind Independence Hall. The circulars for that meeting featured pictures of the cracked Liberty Bell. Several days later, Independence Square was jammed with people coming to hear speakers, such as clergyman Henry Ward Beecher, exhorting everyone to join the fight to put an end to slavery. The speakers' platform was decked in red, white, and blue and featured a large picture of the Liberty Bell.

People all over the country who wanted to end slavery started displaying pictures of the Liberty Bell. Then in 1861 the Civil War, also known as the War Between the States, began. On January 1, 1863, President Abraham Lincoln signed the Emancipation Proclamation, freeing "persons held as slaves" in the Confederacy. Subsequently, the Constitution was amended to prohibit slavery.

Even though the Liberty Bell could no longer ring, as a symbol it had helped win the important campaign for freedom of the slaves.

In 1876 America had its one-hundredth birthday party, the Centennial Exposition, in Philadelphia. The Liberty Bell was a star attraction there. People came to the exposition from all over the country. When they returned home, they told all their friends that they had seen the Liberty Bell. That helped bring more people to the exposition, many to see the bell.

Although the Civil War had ended in 1865, many people from the South still felt separate from the United States. In 1885 the commissioner of the World's Industrial and Cotton Exposition, to be held in New Orleans, wrote Philadelphia's mayor, "Our [Southern] ancestors fought and bled for the time enduring principles [for] which the bell rang out [in] . . . 1776, and, although the bell is the property of the City of Philadelphia, yet are we not co-inheritors of its glories? . . . We ask you to let it come to New Orleans."

Philadelphia's mayor agreed, writing, "The Old Bell . . . by its presence . . . can be the means of . . . cementing harmony through-out the nation," so he shipped it to New Orleans. Consequently, the Liberty Bell became a traveling ambassador of goodwill. The Liberty Bell went to New Orleans, to Charleston, to Boston, in all to fifteen cities to help reunify America. The bell reminded everyone that Americans from the North *and* the South had fought side by side in our War of Independence and that we all believed in liberty. The bell traveled twenty-five thousand miles. It traveled in the open, on its own railroad car, a flatcar. The yoke from which it hung read "1776—proclaim Liberty." Schools and businesses were closed so people could come and see the bell. Whenever the bell was parked in a rail-road yard, thousands of people would gather, some to touch it, others to kiss it or to put flower wreaths on it.

As it paused overnight in Biloxi, Mississippi, Jefferson Davis, ex-president of the Confederacy, rose from his sickbed, went to see the bell, and said, "I believe the time has come when reason should be substituted for passion and when we should be able to do justice to each other. Glorious old Bell, the son of a revolutionary soldier bows in reverence before you."

In 1893 the Liberty Bell went to the World's Columbian

Exposition in Chicago. There and en route, twenty million people visited it. It traveled so much with that great big crack that Philadelphia city officials feared it would fall apart. They ordered a metal spider to be put inside it. Like a true spider, the metal device had legs going out in every direction from its center. The ends of the metal spider's legs were bent into hooks that grasped the bottom edge of the bell and held it together.

In 1915 it finally became possible to telephone across the nation. When the first telephone call was put through, from Philadelphia to San Francisco, a city official tapped the bell with a special wooden mallet. When the sound went out over the telephone wires, the people on the West Coast who heard it must have been thrilled!

Later that year San Francisco planned to hold the Panama-Pacific International Exposition, and its organizers asked Philadelphia city officials to send the Liberty Bell there. Since they were afraid to have the cracked bell travel three thousand miles each way on bumpy rails, the Philadelphians at first refused. However, after two hundred thousand California schoolchildren signed petitions begging Philadelphia to please send the bell, the city relented. When the exposition officials returned the bell, they wrote, "You will be pleased to know that while the Liberty Bell was here in San Francisco, eight million people came to see it!"

That was the last time the Liberty Bell traveled.

But people kept using the Liberty Bell for various other worthy causes.

5.
THE LIBERTY BELL HELPED OTHER IMPORTANT CAUSES

Many people wanted suffrage for women. At first, Susan B. Anthony and Elizabeth Cady Stanton led the crusade. Later, the General Federation of Women's Clubs joined the campaign.

At meetings, suffragists pointed out that women were citizens, just like men; that they were about half the adult population; that they brought up the boys who later became the men; and that most of the schoolteachers who educated the boys were women. So there was no logical reason to keep women from voting.

During the campaign, thousands of people supporting women's suffrage marched to Independence Hall carrying large Liberty Bell banners. Soon suffragists paraded in many cities, displaying such banners.

Since the Liberty Bell could no longer travel, the suffragists ordered a foundry to cast a full-sized replica of the bell, the Woman's Suffrage Liberty Bell. They sent it everywhere as propaganda for women's suffrage. When, in 1920, the Constitution was finally amended to allow women to vote, the suffragists donated the Woman's Suffrage Liberty Bell to the Washington Memorial Chapel in Valley Forge National Historic Park.

Thus, assisted by its traveling replica, the real Liberty Bell had helped win another campaign for American freedom.

For years, many African Americans had been enraged by the regulations that were so humiliating, inconvenient, and unfair to them. Good hotels could not rent rooms to them; good restaurants could not serve them. There were special bathroom and drinking fountain regulations and discriminatory seating rules on buses and in movie theaters.

Finally, a national civil rights movement developed. The civil rights activists wanted equal rights for *all* Americans, regardless of the color of their skin. The Reverend Dr. Martin Luther King, Jr. led that movement. Borrowing from the hymn "America," he made "Let freedom ring" the movement's motto. In 1959 he participated in a wreath-laying ceremony at the Liberty Bell and repeated the motto "Let freedom ring!"

When Congress passed the Civil Rights Act of 1964 our Liberty Bell had helped win yet another American freedom.

6. OUR LIBERTY BELL TODAY

Nowadays, the Liberty Bell is more famous than ever. It is as important a symbol of America as the flag. Today it is in Independence National Historical Park, in Philadelphia. Its presence there is part of the reason that the park was selected as a World Heritage site, the name that celebrates places where "Events of Universal Significance" have taken place.

More than a million people visit the Liberty Bell every year. Even presidents and kings come to see it. Many people take its photograph, and their photos always feature the crack. With a crack showing in a picture of a bell, everyone recognizes it as *the* bell.

The Liberty Bell is so famous now that there are bronze copies of it in each of America's fifty states. State capitols display many of them. Thousands of people have small replicas of the bell in their homes, while others have its picture hanging on their walls. It is featured on American postage stamps and coins. There are even replicas of it in Tokyo, Japan, and Tel Aviv, Israel.

Although it cannot ring, its sound is louder than ever. It now speaks to people all around the world, even in those countries

where people are oppressed and have no liberty. It inspires them to fight for freedom.

Our Liberty Bell speaks to all Americans. It prompts us to be proud of our religious freedom and our civil rights, our democracy and our liberty! It reminds us of the many campaigns it took to gain those liberties and tells us that it is every citizen's duty to keep these liberties alive forever.

GLOSSARY

abolitionists: People working to end slavery

activists: People working hard for a cause

ambassador: Someone who speaks for a foreign government

amend: Change to make better

assemble: Call together; meet

assembly: A gathering of people to make laws, to worship, or to be entertained

assignment: A task

bellman: Someone who rings a bell

campaign: Several battles

cast: To form into a special shape using a mold

centennial: Hundred-year period

charter: A grant of rights

congress: A meeting of representatives

constitution: Basic laws of a nation

continent: One of Earth's main landmasses

craftsman: An expert worker

criticize: To find fault with

crucible: A clay pot that will not melt when heated

declaration: An announcement

delegate: Someone entitled to act for others

device: A tool or machine

dirge: A mournful hymn

display: Show

emotionally: With feeling

exhort: Encourage; stir up

exposition: A show

fuse: Combine

heritage: Tradition

hoist: Pull up

inscription: Something printed or engraved as a lasting record

liberties: Freedoms

notable: Famous; important

patriot: Someone who loves his or her country

privilege: A right granted as a favor

produce: Make

propaganda: An argument for a cause

replica: A copy

representation: Standing for a group

reunify: Bring together again

siege: A continuing effort to force a surrender

significance: Importance

suffrage: The right to vote

suffragists: People working to let women vote

symbol: A sign; an emblem representing something

void: An empty space

yoke: A wood piece from which to hang a bell

Author's Note

Henry Jonas Magaziner, the author, was for many years the regional historical architect and architectural historian for the National Park Service. One of the twenty-eight parks with which he was involved was Independence National Historical Park, the home of the Liberty Bell. His office was near the bell, so he often visited it and listened to the questions that children asked about it. *Our Liberty Bell* is the result.

He checked virtually all the historical facts about the bell against the exhaustive historical study, *The Liberty Bell of Independence National Historical Park*, by National Park Service historian John C. Paige. Former Park Service historian David Kimball provided valuable constructive criticism.

Mr. Magaziner is a Fellow of the American Institute of Architects and the recipient of various awards, including the Presidential Award for Good Design for the Government and the John Harbeson Award for Contributions to the Architectural Profession. He is the author of the architectural book *The Golden Age of Ironwork* (Ocean Pines, Md.: Skipjack Press, 2000).

INDEX

abolitionists, 21, 22, 30
Adams, John, 13, 14
Allen's Town (Allentown), Pennsylvania, 15, 16
Anthony, Susan B., 26
army, Continental, 12, 14, 15
Attucks, Crispus, 10

Beecher, Henry Ward, 22
bell makers, 5, 7
Boston Massacre, 10
Boston Tea Party, 10–11
Brandywine (Pennsylvania), battle of, 15

Carpenters' Hall, 11
Charter of Privileges, 5, 6
Civil War, 23
colonies, thirteen, 5, 10, 11, 12, 13, 14, 17
Constitution (U.S.), 18–19, 23, 26
Continental Congress, First, 11
Continental Congress, Second, 12
Cornwallis, Lord Charles, 17
crucible, 7, 8, 30

Davis, Jefferson, 24

E Pluribus Unum, 14

flag, U.S., 14–15, 28
Franklin, Benjamin, 9, 14, 18
French and Indian War, 9

George III, King, 11, 12, 13, 14

Hamilton, Alexander, 18, 22
Hancock, John, 13
Henry, Patrick, 11, 12
Howe, William, 15

Independence, Declaration of, 12–13, 14, 20, 22
Independence, War of, 11, 14, 15–16, 17, 24
Independence Hall, 20, 21, 22, 26
Independence National Historical Park, 28, 31
Independence Square, 22

Jefferson, Thomas, 12, 14, 19

King, Dr. Martin Luther, Jr., 27

Lee, Henry, 19

Lexington, Massachusetts, 11
Liberty Bell
    and antislavery movement, 21–23
    and civil rights movement, 27
    cracking of, 6, 21
    and first phone call, 25
    hiding of, 15–16
    inscription on, 6, 7, 8, 19, 20, 21
    making of, 7–8
    naming of, 20
    replicas of, 26–27, 29
    ringing of to signal important events, 6, 9, 10, 11, 12, 13–14, 17, 18, 19, 21
    sound of, 6, 8
    traveling of, 23–25
    and women's suffrage movement, 26–27
Lincoln, Abraham, 23
Louisiana Purchase, 19

Madison, James, 18
Morris, Robert, 18

Norris, Isaac, 5, 6

Paoli (Pennsylvania), battle of, 15
Pass, John, 7, 8
Patriots, 11, 12, 13, 14, 15, 16, 30
Penn, William, 5
Pennsylvania Assembly, 5, 6, 8, 9, 17
Pennsylvania State House, 6, 8, 10, 12, 14, 15, 17, 19, 20
Philadelphia, Pennsylvania, 5, 6, 9, 10, 11, 12, 14, 15, 16, 18, 19, 20, 21, 23, 25, 28

Revere, Paul, 10

Saratoga (New York), battle of, 16
Stamp Act, 9
Stanton, Elizabeth Cady, 26
Stow, John, 7, 8
Sugar Act, 9

taxes, 9, 10, 13
Tories, 12, 16
Trenton, New Jersey, 14

Washington, George, 12, 14, 18, 19, 21

Yorktown, Virginia, 17